D0177751

Pieter
BRUEGEL
THE ELDER

Damian Harvey

Illustrated by Yuliya Somina

Contents

CHAPTER 1
A Peasant's Life

Pieter Bruegel was a great artist but his life is a bit of a mystery. It is thought that he was born in 1525, near the Dutch town of Breda in the Netherlands.

One thing about Pieter's early life is certain. His mother and father were farm workers. They didn't have much money and they probably couldn't read or write.

As a young boy, Pieter helped
his parents gather the crops,
plant seeds and tend to the
animals. Pieter didn't want to
spend his life as a peasant.
He dreamt of other things.

As soon as he was old enough, Pieter bravely set out into the world. He'd made up his mind that he wanted to be an artist. Leaving his parents behind, he arrived in the city of Antwerp, in Belgium.

With its busy port, Antwerp was
one of the most important cities in
Europe. Merchants from around the
world travelled there to trade with
each other.

Pieter was sure he could get a job
in such a busy place, and then he
could learn to be an artist.

As well as a being a busy place for merchants, the city of Antwerp had started to attract artists from all over Europe. Wherever there were wealthy merchants, there were people with money to buy paintings.

Pieter was strong from all the farm work he had done. He was sure he could get work loading and unloading ship's cargo if he had to. But first he wandered the city streets and visited as many artist's studios as he could find.

When he visited the studio of a Master called Pieter Coecke van Aelst, the artist agreed to give him a job as an apprentice. Pieter could hardly believe his luck. It was just what he had wanted.

Pieter knew that he would have
to work hard in his Master's studio
with the other young artists, but he
was sure that it wouldn't be as hard
as working on the farm. And it also
meant he would learn how to paint.

CHAPTER 2
Apprentice Artist

Most other apprentices were sons of wealthy merchants or shopkeepers. Pieter wasn't sure he would fit in, and being apprentice to a Master wasn't as easy as he'd imagined.

Pieter worked hard all day. He swept floors, cleaned brushes and made paints by mixing and grinding different natural materials. He also prepared wooden panels for the artists to paint on.

Sometimes he collected supplies from shops around the city and his Master's daughter, Mayken, would go with him.

The Master was impressed by how quickly his apprentice learnt. Soon he was asking young Pieter to help paint pieces of proper artwork.

At first, Pieter painted backgrounds and smaller figures, while his Master worked on the more important details. Pieter's artistic skills soon became clear for everyone to see.

In order to become a Master, Pieter would need to show he had learnt to paint as well as his Master. The artist's studio was an important place to learn and train, and help complete a 'Masterpiece' painting.

In 1551, after studying for five or six years, Pieter Bruegel was accepted as a Master artist by the Guild of St Luke in Antwerp. Now he could open his own studio and take on his own apprentices.

At this time, lots of people were talking about the paintings of Italian artists such as Raphael, Leonardo da Vinci, and Michelangelo, who had painted the ceiling of the Sistine Chapel in Rome.

Pieter wanted to see their work for himself, but not to copy them like other artists. He was determined to find a unique style of his own.

Packing his art materials, Pieter set off on a journey of discovery. He wanted to see people and places he had never seen before.

His trip took him hundreds of miles across the Alps, through Italy...

...and to the Mediterranean Sea.

There were no cars or buses, so
Pieter had to walk or catch rides
with passing merchants. At night he
slept anywhere - in fields,
cattle sheds and with friendly
peasant families.

Pieter stopped to sketch interesting
things that caught his eye such as
mountains and rivers, villages and
people. He visited the Colosseum
in Rome and saw great art. He
sketched war ships fighting on
the sea. He saw lots of beautiful
things but also war and cruelty.

At this time the Netherlands was ruled by Spain and soldiers punished people that didn't do what the Spanish King wanted.

Pieter knew all these things would make his paintings more real. When he finally returned to Antwerp at the end of 1553, Pieter was eager to get to work.

CHAPTER 3
The Print Shop

Pieter went to work for an artist
and printmaker called Hieronymus
Cock. He and his wife owned a shop
in Antwerp called 'At the Sign Of
The Four Winds'.

Hieronymus paid people to copy
works of art so he could make
prints of them. The shop was very
successful and people travelled far
to buy his prints.

As well as selling prints of famous paintings by great Italian artists like Raphael, Hieronymus also wanted customers to be able to buy new pictures by local Dutch artists. This would be Pieter's job.

Landscapes were very popular subjects at the print shop. Pieter's landscapes were often of made-up places, but he used the drawings that he had made on his travels to make them look realistic and interesting.

Strange creatures and demons were also popular in the shop. A Dutch artist called Hieronymus Bosch was famous for his paintings of strange creatures. Pieter found Bosch's style fascinating and he liked to use some of his techniques in his own artwork.

Making a living as an artist could be very hard. Most artists had to rely on wealthy people paying them. The rich would often ask an artist to paint pictures of their families, their houses or their pets.

Pieter didn't want to spend his life just painting rich people so he was happy working for Hieronymus Cock. While doing prints, he was able to develop his own artistic style in his studio and still earn money.

Pieter wanted his pictures to be fun and entertaining, so he filled them with details and interesting people. At first he drew most of them using a pen and brown ink, and signed them with his name, 'Brueghel'.

Pieter's pictures were popular in
Hieronymus Cock's print shop and
people were eager to buy more but
he didn't want to use pen and ink all
the time. He wanted to paint with
oils and be recognised for his skill.

CHAPTER 4
A Master

When he was 39 years old, Pieter painted a picture called 'The Fight Between Carnival and Lent'. Set in a town square, the painting is bright and full of colour.

It shows people feasting and fasting, eating and drinking. Children and adults play games in the street while others are working, begging or going to church to pray.

Pieter was so happy with the painting that he dated it (1559) and signed it 'Bruegel' instead of 'Brueghel'. No one is sure why he changed his name but perhaps, now he had found his own style, he wanted to make a name for himself in the world of art.

Pieter had finally achieved his dream of becoming a Master artist. He loved painting in his studio and he enjoyed sharing his skills with the young artists that came to see him.

He took his painting very seriously but he also laughed and joked with his students. Sometimes he told them scary stories that he had heard when he was growing up.

Bruegel became known for various techniques like foreshortening. He used dark brown colours at the front or foreground, green in the middle and light blue in the background.

For landscapes he would often add
a viewpoint which brought his
paintings to life. Each one was full
of many tiny details and told a story.
His work became more and more
popular.

But Pieter was not completely
happy. He was looking for love
as well as fame.

One day, Pieter remembered Mayken Coecke van Aelst, the daughter of his old Master. He remembered how well they had got on while collecting art supplies.

Pieter travelled to Brussels, where Mayken now lived, to ask her to be his wife. Mayken was delighted but her mother said that, if Pieter wanted to marry her daughter, he would have to give up his studio in Antwerp and move to Brussels. Pieter agreed and, in 1563, the two were married.

CHAPTER 5
Peasant Painter

Pieter was happier now than he had been in his whole life. Over the next few years he worked harder than ever and painted his most famous and popular paintings.

Instead of painting wealthy people, Pieter filled many of his paintings with the peasants and workers and scenes from their everyday lives in towns and villages.

Sometimes he disguised himself as a peasant and pretended to be a guest at a wedding. There, Pieter watched people and used them in his paintings.

In 1565, Nicolaas Jonghelinck, a wealthy merchant friend of Pieter's, paid him to paint six new pictures.

Pieter created six paintings of landscapes to show the changing seasons. In some he included people gathering crops, working on the land and herding cattle. In another he painted hunters trudging through the snow while people skated and played on the frozen river.

Pieter and Mayken had two sons, Pieter and Jan. Both of them grew into artists and they too had sons who became artists.

Pieter the Younger copied a lot of his father's paintings. Jan became known for his talent for painting flowers.

Sadly, Pieter never saw his sons paint. He died at the age of 44, when they were still very young, and was buried at Notre-Dame de la Chappelle in Brussels.

In the years after Pieter died, a lot of people forgot about him and some of his pictures were lost. Because he painted the everyday life of peasants, some people thought his paintings couldn't be very good or important. They even nicknamed him 'Peasant Bruegel'.

It was a long time before people looked at his paintings again and realised how important he was. Instead of just painting rich lords and ladies, Pieter Bruegel had captured the lives of everyday people in a way that no one else had. He was a real Master.

Timeline

1525~ 1530 Bruegel is born in Breda, Netherlands.

1545 Pieter becomes an apprentice for Pieter Coecke van Aelst.

1551 Pieter is acknowledged as a 'Master' by the Painters' Guild in Antwerp.

1554 Pieter starts working in Hieronymus Cock's print shop, 'At the Sign of the Four Winds'.

1559 Pieter paints 'The Fight Between Carnival and Lent' and changes his name from Brueghel to Bruegel.

1563	Pieter moves to Brussels and marries Mayken Coecke van Aelst.
1564	Pieter and Mayken's first son is born. They name him Pieter (the Younger).
1565	Pieter paints a series of 6 pictures of the Seasons for a wealthy merchant, Nicolaas Jonghelinck.
1568	Pieter and Mayken's second son, Jan, is born.
1569	Pieter dies and is buried at Notre-Dame de la Chapelle in Brussels.

Website links

http://www.pieter-bruegel-the-elder.org

http://www.wikiart.org/en/pieter-bruegel-the-elder

First published in 2014 by
Franklin Watts
338 Euston Road
London NW1 3BH

Franklin Watts Australia
Level 17/207 Kent Street
Sydney NSW 2000

HB ISBN 978 1 4451 3311 9
PB ISBN 978 1 4451 3315 7
Library ebook ISBN 978 1 4451 3317 1
ebook ISBN 978 1 4451 3318 8

Dewey Decimal Classification Number: 759.9'493

Series editor: Melanie Palmer
Series designer Cathryn Gilbert

Printed in Great Britain

Franklin Watts is a division of Hachette Children's Books,
an Hachette UK company.
www.hachette.co.uk

Advisory note to parents and teachers: every effort has been made by
the Publishers to ensure that the websites are suitable for children and
that they contain no inappropriate or offensive material. However,
beacuse of the nature of the Internet, it is impossible to gurantee that
the contents of these sites will not be altered. We strongly advise that
Internet access is supervised by a responsible adult.